A LOOK AT SPACE SCIENCE

THE SUN AND OTHER STARS

BY BERT WILBERFORCE

Gareth Stevens
PUBLISHING

CRASHCOURSE

Please visit our website, www.garethstevens.com. For a free color catalog of all our high-quality books, call toll free 1-800-542-2595 or fax 1-877-542-2596.

Library of Congress Cataloging-in-Publication Data
Names: Wilberforce, Bert, author.
Title: The sun and other stars / Bert Wilberforce.
Description: New York : Gareth Stevens Publishing, [2021] | Series: A look
   at space science | Includes bibliographical references and index. |
   Contents: Our sun, our star -- Ball of gases -- The sun's size -- So
   hot! -- Solar wind -- Star sizes, star colors -- Our star is born --
   Supernova! -- Recycling stars -- The Life cycles of stars.
Identifiers: LCCN 2019050763 | ISBN 9781538259245 (library binding) | ISBN
   9781538259221 (paperback) | ISBN 9781538259238 | ISBN 9781538259252
   (ebook)
Subjects: LCSH: Stars--Juvenile literature. | Sun--Juvenile literature.
Classification: LCC QB521.5 .W55 2021 | DDC 523.8--dc23
LC record available at https://lccn.loc.gov/2019050763

First Edition

Published in 2021 by
Gareth Stevens Publishing
111 East 14th Street, Suite 349
New York, NY 10003

Designer: Sarah Liddell
Editor: Therese Shea

Photo credits: Cover, p. 1 (main) Aphelleon/Shutterstock.com; background used throughout Zakharchuk/Shutterstock.com; p. 5 Edmund O'Connor/Shutterstock.com; p. 7 (main) khak/Shutterstock.com; p. 7 (diagram) Nasky/Shutterstock.com; p. 9 Withan Tor/Shutterstock.com; p. 11 Nepster/Shutterstock.com; p. 13 janez volmajer/Shutterstock.com; p. 15 Krissanapong Wongsawarng/Shutterstock.com; p. 17 sripfoto/Shutterstock.com; p. 19 Astrobobo/Shutterstock.com; p. 21 Ron Miller/Stocktrek Images/Stocktrek Images/Getty Images; p. 23 McCarthy's PhotoWorks/Shutterstock.com; p. 25 NASA images/Shutterstock.com; p. 27 Allexxandar/Shutterstock.com; p. 29 ComputerHotline/Wikimedia Commons; p. 30 VectorMine/Shutterstock.com.

Printed in the United States of America

Some of the images in this book illustrate individuals who are models. The depictions do not imply actual situations or events.

CPSIA compliance information: Batch #CS20GS: For further information contact Gareth Stevens, New York, New York at 1-800-542-2595.

Find us on 🅵 🅾

CONTENTS

Words in the glossary appear in **bold** type the first time they are used in the text.

OUR SUN, OUR STAR

Our sun is a star. Without the sun's light, Earth would be dark. Without the sun's heat, Earth would be cold. Plants wouldn't grow. We couldn't live. Earth would fly off into space! Where does the sun's power come from? Read on!

MAKE THE GRADE

The sun gives us heat and light. People have found ways to make **electricity** from solar energy, or power, too! Solar means "from the sun."

BALL OF GASES

The sun and other stars are made up mostly of the gases hydrogen and helium. In the sun's core, or center, great **pressure** causes hydrogen atoms to come together and form helium atoms. This **process** gives off a huge amount of energy.

CORE

HYDROGEN 71%

HELIUM 27%

OTHER 2%

MAKE THE GRADE
The process of atoms joining to make
new atoms is called nuclear fusion.

THE SUN'S SIZE

The **diameter** of the sun is about 864,000 miles (1,390,500 km). It's about 2,715,395 miles (4,370,005 km) around the sun. It would take about 332,946 Earths to equal the sun's mass, or amount of matter. Over 1 **million** Earths could fit inside it!

MAKE THE GRADE

Our solar system is the sun and
all the space objects that orbit it.
The sun has more than 99 percent of
all the mass in our solar system!

Objects with mass have gravity, which is the force that pulls objects toward other objects. Larger objects have more gravity. The sun has so much mass that everything in our solar system is kept in **orbit** by its gravity!

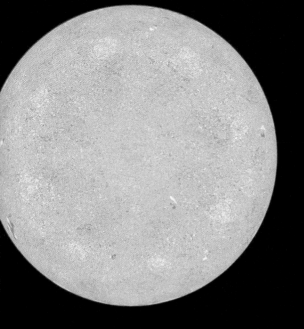

EARTH

MAKE THE GRADE

Earth is about 93 million miles
(150 million km) from the sun. It doesn't
orbit the sun in an exact circle. Sometimes
it's a bit closer or farther away from it.

SO HOT!

At the sun's core, the **temperature** is about 27,000,000°F (15,000,000°C). The sun's **surface**, or photosphere, is about 10,000°F (5,500°C). The energy from the core travels to the photosphere very slowly. It may take as long as a million years!

MAKE THE GRADE

It only takes about 8 minutes for light from the photosphere to reach Earth.

MAKE THE GRADE

Auroras happen on Jupiter,
Saturn, Uranus, and Neptune too!

STAR SIZES, STAR COLORS

You might think the sun is a large star. It looks so much bigger than the other stars in the night sky. However, there are stars much larger and much smaller than our sun. They're all so far away that they look tiny.

MAKE THE GRADE
The largest stars are called hypergiants.
The smallest are called red dwarfs.

Stars can be different colors. These colors give us clues about how hot the star burns. The hottest stars are blueish. The coolest stars are reddish. Our sun looks white, and its surface temperature lies between these two kinds of stars.

MAKE THE GRADE

The surface of the red star Betelgeuse is about 5,800°F (3,200°C). The surface of the blue star Rigel is about 19,300°F (10,700°C).

BETELGEUSE

RIGEL

Our sun is called a yellow dwarf star because of its size and color. Red supergiants can be more than 100 times the diameter of the sun. White dwarfs are much smaller than the sun, or about the size of Earth.

MAKE THE GRADE

Antares is a red supergiant star.
You can see how much larger it is
than our sun in this picture. There
are even larger stars, though!

BETA CENTAURI

VEGA

THE SUN

ALDEBARAN

ANTARES

ARCTURUS

OUR STAR IS BORN

Like all stars, our sun formed in a cloud of gas and dust called a nebula. Forces caused matter in the nebula to come together. A hot core of dust and gas called a protostar formed. It became our sun.

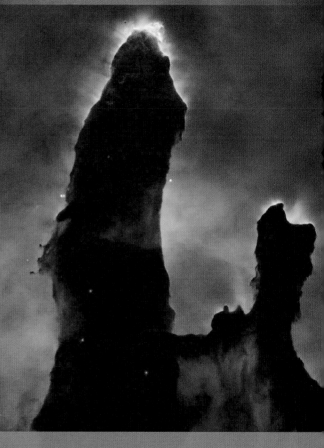

MESSIER 16, A STAR-FORMING NEBULA

MAKE THE GRADE

Our sun is about 4½ **billion** years old. Scientists think it will burn for about 5 billion more years!

When the sun dies, it will burn brightly as a red giant. Then, it will become a smaller white dwarf with a shell of gas around it. This is called a planetary nebula. Finally, the white dwarf will burn out and become a black dwarf.

MAKE THE GRADE

When the sun's hydrogen is almost gone, it will be left with a helium core. The helium will heat up and collapse, or cave in. This creates the light and heat of a red giant star.

MAKE THE GRADE

Some collapsed stars form black holes. These are places with a powerful force of gravity that draws in all matter that gets close, even light!

27

RECYCLING STARS

When stars explode, they give off matter that mixes with gas and dust in space. This is the matter that makes new stars and new star systems. In this way, stars recycle matter. Scientists learn more surprising star facts every day!

MAKE THE GRADE

Scientists have found that many star systems hold two stars that orbit each other, such as the Kepler-47 system.

29

THE LIFE CYCLES OF STARS

HIGH-MASS STAR

LOW-MASS OR MEDIUM-MASS STAR

RED SUPERGIANT

RED GIANT

STAR-FORMING NEBULA

SUPERNOVA

PLANETARY NEBULA

NEUTRON STAR

WHITE DWARF

BLACK HOLE

GLOSSARY

billion: 1,000 million, or 1,000,000,000

diameter: the distance from one side of a round object to another through its center

electricity: a form of power carried through wires and used to operate machines

element: matter, such as hydrogen, that is pure and has no other type of matter in it

explode: to break apart suddenly and with great force

magnetic field: the area around a magnet where its pull is felt. Earth has a magnetic field too.

million: 1,000 thousand, or 1,000,000

neutron: a very small particle of matter with no electrical charge that's part of almost all atoms

orbit: to travel in a circle or oval around something, or the path used to make that trip

particle: a very small piece of something

pressure: a force that pushes on something else

process: a series of steps or actions to complete something

surface: the top layer of a planet, star, or other space object

temperature: how hot or cold something is

FOR MORE INFORMATION

BOOKS

Crane, Cody. *The Stars*. New York, NY: Children's Press, 2018.

Rathburn, Betsy. *The Sun*. Minneapolis, MN: Bellwether Media, 2019.

WEBSITES

Star Facts for Kids
www.sciencekids.co.nz/sciencefacts/space/stars.html
Read a collection of fun star facts.

Sun
spaceplace.nasa.gov/menu/sun/
Find many answers to your sun questions.

INDEX